Table of Contents

Introduction to Journal Writing: Grade 3

Introduction

Writing is a basic form of communication that requires instruction and practice. Students constantly need to engage in a variety of writing experiences, from vocabulary development to creative expression, to become competent communicators. Research shows that the more students practice and experience written communication, the more highly developed their skills will be. Moreover, they often become more prolific writers. Even when faced with a limited vocabulary or basic writing skills, students who are encouraged to create stories through drawing or dictation seem to have a more positive attitude toward communicating through a written language.

The activity pages in *Introduction to Journal Writing Grade 3* encourage students to practice writing in a fun, creative way. The pages are designed to accommodate a variety of writing levels. Students may respond with a single word, a phrase, a sentence, a paragraph, and through illustrations. The pages are structured to provide a successful writing experience for each student, while allowing for personal response.

Organization

Introduction to Journal Writing Grade 3 is divided into two parts. The first part has eight units, which deal with such themes as me, friends, animals, and shopping. Each of these units has eight activity sheets. The second part of *Introduction to Journal Writing Grade 3* is a 26-page Personal Dictionary that can be photocopied for students so they can list words that are special or interesting to them.

Use

Students do not need additional instruction to complete any of the pages in this book. Copies of the activity sheets can be given to individuals, pairs of students, or small groups for completion. They can also be used as a center activity.

To begin, determine the implementation that best fits your students' needs and your classroom structure. You may wish to use the following ideas:

- Introduce students to the purpose of writing. Point out that the pages can help develop the writing skills of a bigger vocabulary and a focus on detail, as well as provide creative writing ideas.
- Remind students there is no right or wrong answer.
- For beginning writers or students needing additional help, pair children with a "writing buddy," perhaps an older or more advanced student. This student could read the page to the writer, as well as take dictation in order to free the writer for creative expression. The buddy could then read the page back and encourage the writer to read the page.
- Encourage children to maintain a Writer's Notebook. In it they can write or draw ideas for stories they gather from the activity pages.
- Encourage students to share their writings with the class, either verbally, by displaying completed sheets on a bulletin board, or by binding the unit pages to make individual books.

Additional Notes

PARENT LETTER: Send the Letter to Parents home with students.

CURRICULUM CORRELATION: A chart on page 4 identifies subject areas in which the pages could be incorporated into your daily lesson plans.

STUDENT PROGRESS CHARTS: Duplicate the grid sheets found on pages 5 and 6. Record students' names in the left column. Note when students have completed each activity page.

PERSONAL DICTIONARY: Beginning on page 71, you will find a 26-page Personal Dictionary. Photocopy the pages for the students and have them make a cover for their book. Encourage students to keep a list of words they use often or find interesting. Have them store their dictionary in their desk for easy reference or in a conveniently placed file.

Name _____ Date _____

My List

Things I build:

_____

_____

_____

Things I swing on:

_____

_____

_____

Tricks I know:

_____

_____

_____

Things I munch:

_____

_____

_____

People who hug me:

_____

_____

_____

Name _____   Date _____

My Busy Day

7:00 A.M.	
8:00 A.M.	
11:00 A.M.	
3:00 P.M.	
5:00 P.M.	
6:00 P.M.	
8:00 P.M.	

Have students complete this chart over the course of the day.

Unit 1: Just Me!

Name _____   Date _____

Words Say It All!

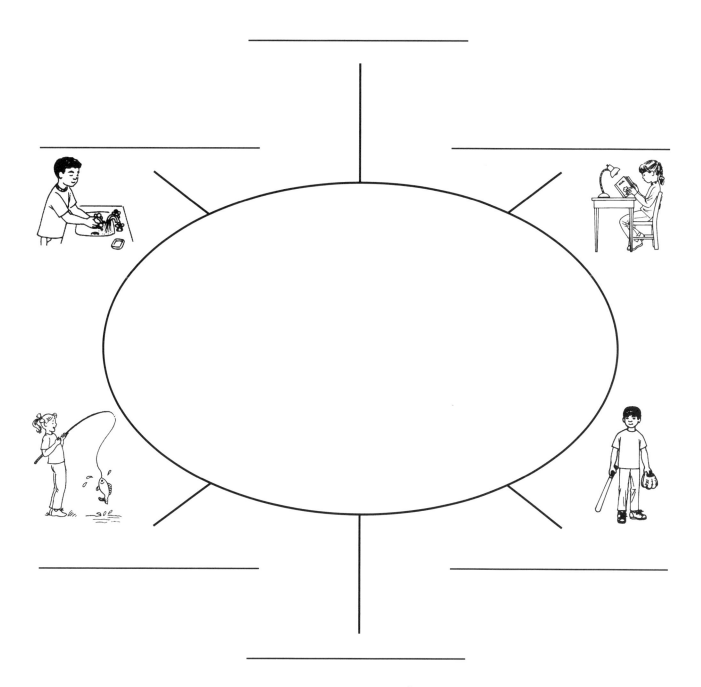

Have students draw self-portraits and then write words that describe themselves.

© Steck-Vaughn Company   9   **Unit 1: Just Me!**

Journal Writing 3, SV 5799-3

Name _____ Date _____

Wish Upon a Star

Twinkle, twinkle, little star,
How I wonder what you are.
Up above the moon so high,
Like a diamond in the sky.
Twinkle, twinkle, little star,
How I wonder what you are.

I wish I could _____

_____

_____ .

I wish I had _____

_____

_____ .

I wish _____

_____

_____ .

Name _____   Date _____

Give It Your Best!

Athletes always give their best try. When do you give your best try?

_____

_____

_____

_____

_____

_____

Have students write a paragraph telling about times they try hard to do something. Then they should illustrate it.

Unit 1: Just Me!

© Steck-Vaughn Company   13   Journal Writing 3, SV 5799-3

Now and Later

I am very good at	I really like to
_____	_____
_____	_____
_____	_____

When I grow up, I would like to

_____

_____

_____

_____

_____

_____

_____

Have students complete the lists and then write paragraphs telling what they would like to do when they grow up.

Unit 1: Just Me!

Speaking of friendship

When I meet my friend, my friend says,

_____
_____

At recess, my friend says,

_____
_____

On the phone, my friend says,

_____
_____

On my birthday, my friend says,

_____
_____

When I am mad, my friend says,

_____
_____

Have students fill in the dialogue balloons.

Unit 2: Friendship Ties

Name _____   Date _____

Friendship by the Book

I would like to be friends with

_____

from the book

_____ .

Together, we could _____

_____

_____

_____

_____

_____

_____

_____ .

Have students complete the sentence and write a paragraph telling what activities they would do with the character. Then have students draw a picture of the character.

Unit 2: Friendship Ties

© Steck-Vaughn Company   16   Journal Writing 3, SV 5799-3

Name _____ Date _____

Friendly Letter

Friends I would like to write to	Important news I could share
_____	_____
_____	_____
_____	_____

Dear _____ ,

_____

_____

_____

_____

_____

_____

_____

Have each student complete each list and then write a letter to a friend.

Unit 2: Friendship Ties

Name _____   Date _____

We Like to Be Alike!

I like to eat _____ .

My friend would rather eat _____ .

We both like to eat _____ .

I like to wear _____ .

My friend would rather wear _____ .

We both like to wear _____ .

I like to go _____ .

My friend would rather go _____ .

We both like to go _____ .

Name _____ Date _____

A Friend in Need

There is a new student in your class who does not speak your language. You and the student want to be friends. What can you do together?

_____

_____

_____

_____

_____

_____

_____

_____

_____

_____

_____

Have students each write a paragraph telling ways they could play with someone who did not speak their language.

Unit 2: Friendship Ties

© Steck-Vaughn Company   19   Journal Writing 3, SV 5799-3

Name _____ Date _____

Diagramming a Friendship

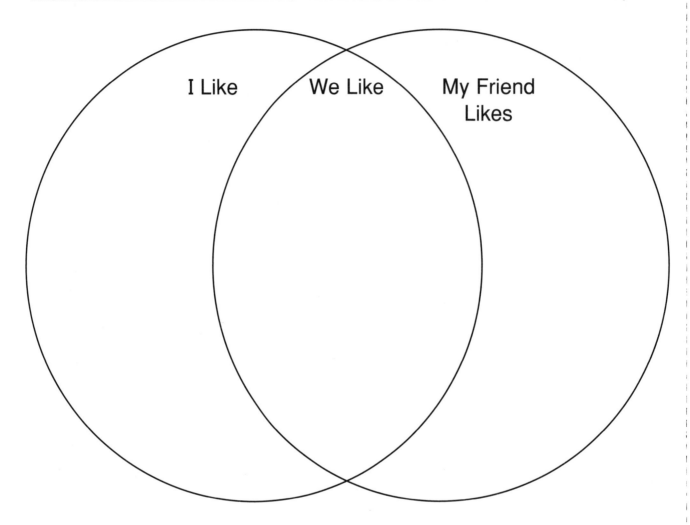

I Like   We Like   My Friend
                                Likes

Have students complete the Venn Diagram.

Unit 2: Friendship Ties

Name _____ Date _____

I Had a Secret

I had a secret,
and told it to a friend,

who told it _____

who _____

who _____
who told EVERYBODY.

Here's the secret:

_____

_____

_____

_____

Words of Friendship

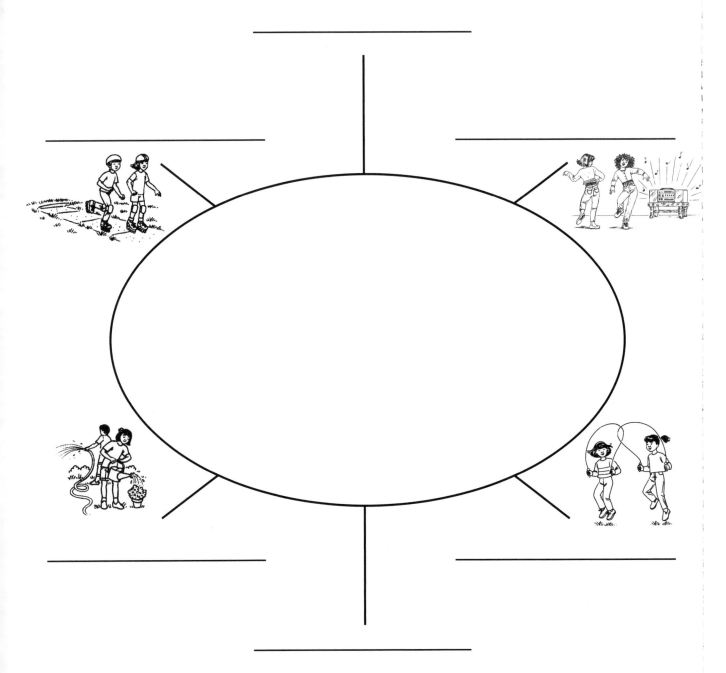

Have students write words that describe characteristics of a good friend.
Then have each student draw a picture illustrating one of the characteristics.

Unit 2: Friendship Ties

© Steck-Vaughn Company   22   Journal Writing 3, SV 5799-3

Name _____   Date _____

Puppy Care

1. Food: _____

_____

2. Exercise: _____

_____

3. Toys: _____

_____

4. Other things you need: _____

_____

5. A good place to sleep: _____

_____

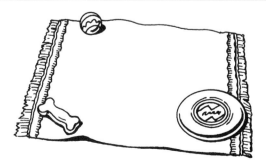

Name _____ Date _____

Marching Home

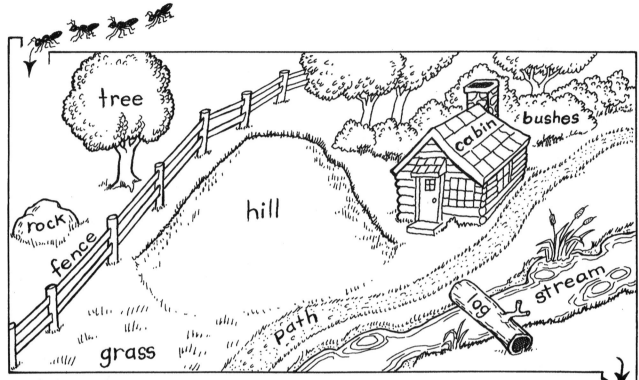

tree

rock

fence

hill

cabin

bushes

grass

path

log

stream

These ants go marching

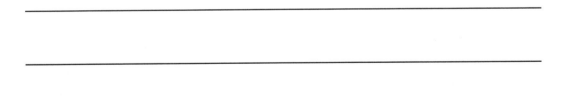

_____

_____

_____

_____

_____

_____

Have students draw a route for a new ants march.
Then describe the route.

Unit 3: Fun with Animals

© Steck-Vaughn Company   24   Journal Writing 3, SV 5799-3

Name _____ Date _____

Another View

Some people think a grasshopper is ugly,
but it is beautiful because

I. _____

_____

2. _____

_____

3. _____

_____

Some people think a kitten is fun,
but it is work because

I. _____

_____

2. _____

_____

3. _____

_____

Have students complete each section.

Unit 3: Fun with Animals

Journal Writing 3, SV 5799-3

Name _____   Date _____

Why the Noise?

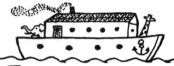

Why did the bee buzz?

Why did the mouse squeak?

Why did the frog croak?

Why did the bear growl?

Have students invent answers to the questions.

© Steck-Vaughn Company

Unit 3: Fun with Animals

Journal Writing 3, SV 5799-3

30

Name _____   Date _____

Adventures Out of This World!

Astronauts explore distant places.
When did you explore an interesting place?

_____

_____

_____

_____

_____

_____

_____

_____

_____

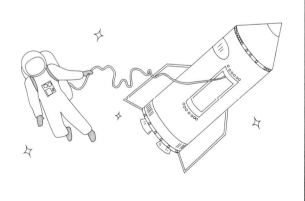

Have students each tell about an interesting place they
visited. Then have them illustrate the paragraph.

Unit 4: On the Go!

© Steck-Vaughn Company   31   Journal Writing 3, SV 5799-3

Name _____   Date _____

A New Way to Go

I would like to ride in a(n) _____ .

Then I could _____

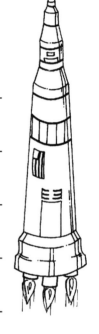

_____

_____

_____

_____

_____

_____

_____

_____

_____

_____ .

Have students each tell about something they would like to ride in. Then have them illustrate the paragraph.

Unit 4: On the Go!

© Steck-Vaughn Company   32   Journal Writing 3, SV 5799-3

Name _____ Date _____

Pack and Go

When I go to _____ ,

I will pack

_____   _____

_____   _____

_____   _____

_____   _____

_____   _____

_____   _____

_____   _____

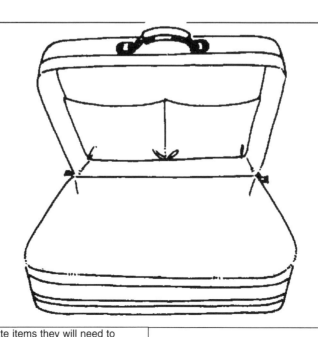

Have students list and illustrate items they will need to take on a trip.

Unit 4: On the Go!

Name _____ Date _____

I Would . . .

At the beach, I would

_____

_____

_____ .

In the mountains, I would

_____

_____

_____ .

In a forest, I would

_____

_____

_____ .

Have students complete and illustrate each sentence.

Unit 4: On the Go!

Name _____ Date _____

Under Water

If I could dive to the bottom of the ocean, I would

_____

_____

_____

_____

_____

_____

_____

_____

_____

Have students each write a paragraph telling what they would like to do during an ocean diving adventure.

Unit 4: On the Go!

Name _____ Date _____

Dear Diary

Dear Diary,

What a wonderful trip to _____ !
Let me tell you all the things we have done.

_____

_____

_____

_____

_____

_____

_____

_____

_____

Have students each choose a place to visit and write a
diary entry telling about activities they could do there.

Name _____ Date _____

Speaking About a Problem!

Suppose you are visiting a foreign country. You do not speak the language, and you are lost. What will you do?

1. _____

_____

2. _____

_____

3. _____

_____

4. _____

_____

Have students complete the list.

Unit 4: On the Go!

Name _____ Date _____

A Magical Ride

If I could ride a magic carpet to any place in the world, I would go to

_____ , because

_____

_____

_____

_____

_____

_____

_____

_____

_____

_____

Name _____ Date _____

Sensing Food

My favorite food is _____

_____ .

It looks _____

_____ .

It smells _____

_____ .

It feels _____

_____ .

It sounds _____

_____ .

It tastes _____

_____ .

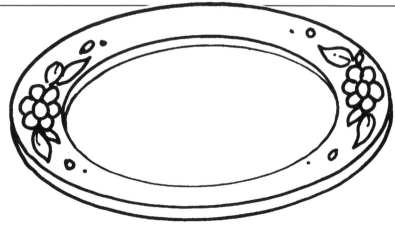

Have each student complete the sentences and draw a
picture showing their favorite food.

Unit 5: My Sense-able World!

Name _____ Date _____

A City Full of Noise

All around the city street,
I hear the noises.
I hear people noises,

_____ and _____ and _____ .

I hear store noises,

_____ and _____ and _____ .

I hear faraway noises,

_____ and _____ and _____ .

Sometimes, I hear _____ and _____ .

Once, I heard _____ .

The city has lots of noises.

Name _____ Date _____

Still Lost!

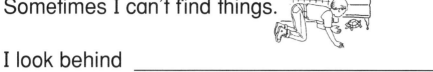

Sometimes I can't find things.

I look behind _____ .

I look under _____ .

I look in _____ .

I look between _____ .

I look on _____ .

I look near _____ .
Sometimes I find them, but sometimes I don't.

Things I have not found:

_____

_____

_____

_____

_____

I will keep looking.

Have students complete the sentences and then list items
they have lost.

Unit 5: My Sense-able World!

© Steck-Vaughn Company

41

Journal Writing 3, SV 5799-3

Name _____ Date _____

A Feeling You Get!

Velvety

_____

_____

_____

_____

Squishy

_____

_____

_____

_____

Prickly

_____

_____

_____

_____

Gooey

_____

_____

_____

_____

Wavy

_____

_____

_____

_____

Have students complete each list with items that have those textures.

Unit 5: My Sense-able World!

Name _____ Date _____

Tasteful Titles

A good recipe name will make someone want to try a recipe.
Choose foods and write words that have the same beginning letter
as the name of the food, such as Simply Super Salad.

1. _____

2. _____

3. _____

Choose one name from above and write a recipe for it.

_____

_____ _____

_____ _____

_____ _____

_____

_____

_____

Name _____ Date _____

The Nose Knows

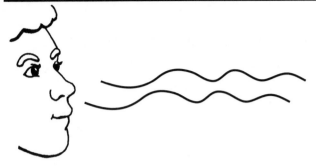

One day I smelled something really _____ .
I decided to follow the smell to see what it was!

_____

_____

_____

_____

_____

_____

_____

_____

_____

Have each student complete the paragraph.

Unit 5: My Sense-able World!

Name _____ Date _____

A Special Place

I have a special place I like to go to be alone!

My special place is _____

_____ .

When I'm there,

I hear _____ ,

I see _____ ,

I taste _____ ,

I smell _____ ,

and I touch _____ .

My place is special because _____

_____

_____

_____

_____ .

Name _____   Date _____

Hide and Seek

Five little dinosaurs,

hiding _____ .

Four singing robins,

hiding _____ .

Three smelly skunks,

hiding _____ .

Two friends with a secret,

hiding _____ .

One _____

hiding _____ .

Have students invent and list possible hiding places and complete the last sentence with their own choices.

Unit 5: My Sense-able World!

© Steck-Vaughn Company   46   Journal Writing 3, SV 5799-3

Name _____   Date _____

Where to Play?

Will the kitten play
in the toy box?
in the garden?
in the leaves?
in the garbage?
in the washing?
EVERYWHERE!

Where will you play?
I will play

_____

_____

_____

_____

_____

Unit 6: Outside Fun

Name _____   Date _____

Lots of Litter

Ways the community can solve
the problem of litter:

_____

_____

_____

_____

I can help solve the problem of litter by

_____

_____

_____

_____

_____

_____

_____

Name _____   Date _____

Seasons of Sports

In the winter, I play

_____

_____ .

In the spring, I play

_____

_____ .

In the summer, I play

_____

_____ .

In the fall, I play

_____

_____ .

Have students complete and illustrate the sentences.

© Steck-Vaughn Company

Unit 6: Outside Fun

Name _____ Date _____

Scavenger Hunt

Long things:

1. _____

2. _____

3. _____

4. _____

Rough things:

1. _____

2. _____

3. _____

4. _____

Round things:

1. _____

2. _____

3. _____

4. _____

Funny things:

1. _____

2. _____

3. _____

4. _____

Have students take a walk outside and complete the lists.

Unit 6: Outside Fun

Name _____   Date _____

Naturally Delicious

I like to make mud sundaes.
Here is my recipe for this treat!

Mud Sundae

What you need:

_____   _____

_____   _____

_____   _____

What you do:

_____

_____

_____

_____

_____

_____

Have children complete the recipe telling how
to make a mud sundae.

Unit 6: Outside Fun

Name _____ Date _____

Playground Talk

Can I play?

Have students fill in the dialogue balloons with comments they might hear on the playground.

Unit 6: Outside Fun

© Steck-Vaughn Company

52

Journal Writing 3, SV 5799-3

Name _____ Date _____

No Matter the Weather!

I go outside in the rain and

_____

_____

_____ .

I go outside in the snow and

_____

_____

_____ .

I go outside on a hot day and

_____

_____

_____ .

Have students complete and illustrate each sentence.

Unit 6: Outside Fun

Name _____   Date _____

A Secret Hideout

I am going to build a secret hideout in the woods.
Here is what I will need to do to make the hideout.

_____

_____

_____

_____

_____

_____

_____

Have students write a paragraph telling what materials and
tools they will need and how they will build a hideout.

Unit 6: Outside Fun

© Steck-Vaughn Company   54   Journal Writing 3, SV 5799-3

Name _____ Date _____

For Sale Signs

At the pet store

At the supermarket

At the ice cream store

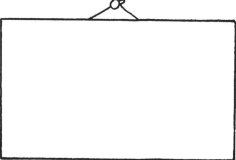

At the toy store

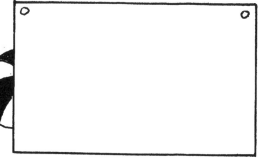

Name _____   Date _____

Sell It "Write" Away

The Times

[picture box]

_____

_____

_____

_____

_____

_____

_____

_____

_____

_____

_____

_____

Have students each draw a picture of an item they would
like to sell. Then have them write a sales ad.

Unit 7: What's in Store?

© Steck-Vaughn Company   56   Journal Writing 3, SV 5799-3

Name _____ Date _____

Color Buys

My favorite color is _____ .

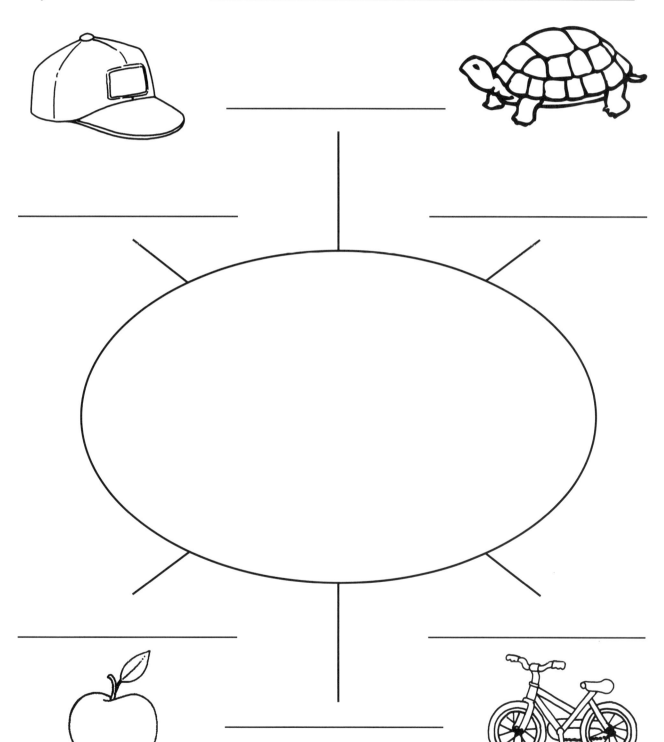

Unit 7: What's in Store?

Name _____   Date _____

What Would You Say?

Have students fill in the dialogue balloons with comments each person might say.

Unit 7: What's in Store?

© Steck-Vaughn Company

Journal Writing 3, SV 5799-3

Name _____ Date _____

The Reasons Why

I really want to buy _____, but Mom says "No!"

Here is a list of really good reasons she should change her mind!

1. _____

    _____

2. _____

    _____

3. _____

    _____

4. _____

    _____

Have each student write a list of things to say or do to change a mother's mind about buying something.

Unit 7: What's in Store?

© Steck-Vaughn Company 59 Journal Writing 3, SV 5799-3

Name _____   Date _____

Shopping Spree

If I had $1,000, I would

_____

_____

_____

_____

_____

_____

_____

 Have students each write a paragraph telling what they would do with a large sum of money. Then have them illustrate the paragraph.

© Steck-Vaughn Company   60   Journal Writing 3, SV 5799-3

Unit 7: What's in Store?

No Choice!

You wouldn't believe what my mom made me buy!

_____

_____

_____

_____

_____

_____

_____

_____

Have students each write a paragraph telling about
something they bought that they did not like.

Unit 7: What's in Store?

Name _____ Date _____

Working Out

I would like to work in a _____ store,

because _____

_____

_____

_____

_____

_____

_____

_____

_____

_____

Have students each choose a store and tell why they would like to work in it.

Unit 7: What's in Store?

Name _____ Date _____

A Character to Remember

My favorite storybook character is _____.

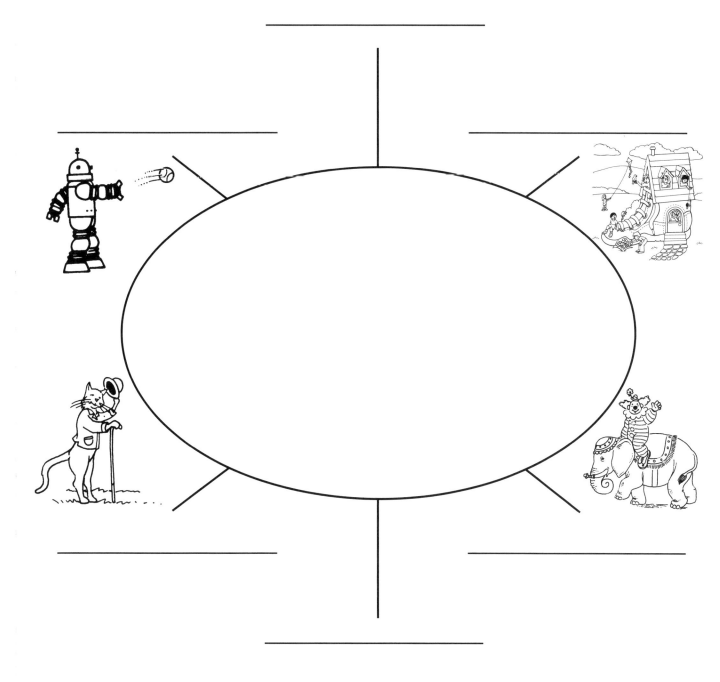

Have each student draw a picture of a favorite character and describe the character.

Unit 8: Over the Rainbow

© Steck-Vaughn Company

63

Journal Writing 3, SV 5799-3

Name _____ Date _____

I Can't See the Problem!

One day I got a drink from the kitchen. I felt funny! When I went to the bathroom, I looked in the mirror. I couldn't believe what I saw. I could see my clothes, but I could not see my face!

_____

_____

_____

_____

_____

_____

_____

_____

_____

_____

Have students each write a paragraph telling what they would do if they were invisible.

Unit 8: Over the Rainbow

© Steck-Vaughn Company   64   Journal Writing 3, SV 5799-3

Name _____ Date _____

The Princess and the Swan

One day a princess
was going to town.
She got lost.
A swan found the princess and
decided to help her.
The princess flew home on the back of the swan.
The swan changed into a prince.
The prince and the princess became friends.

And then, _____

_____

_____

_____

_____

Have students read and continue the story.

Name _____   Date _____

My Fairy Tale

Once upon a time,

_____

Name _____ Date _____

Animal Play

Animals	Rhyming Words	Rhyming Sentence
snake	rake, bake, lake	The snake had a rake by the lake.

Have students complete the table and illustrate several sentences.

It Smells Like Friendship

Smelly the Skunk goes to school, but no one wants to be his friend. Smelly thinks of a plan to make friends.

_____

_____

_____

_____

_____

_____

_____

_____

_____

_____

_____

_____

Have each student complete a paragraph telling how a skunk makes friends.

Unit 8: Over the Rainbow

© Steck-Vaughn Company   68   Journal Writing 3, SV 5799-3

Name _____   Date _____

Squeaking By

An elephant and a mouse become friends. When the mouse visits the elephant, there are some big problems.

_____

_____

_____

_____

_____

_____

_____

_____

_____

Have each student complete a paragraph telling about a time a mouse visits an elephant.

Unit 8: Over the Rainbow

© Steck-Vaughn Company   69   Journal Writing 3, SV 5799-3

Wishful Thinking

If a wizard gives me three wishes,
I will wish for

1. _____

   _____

2. _____

   _____

3. _____

   _____

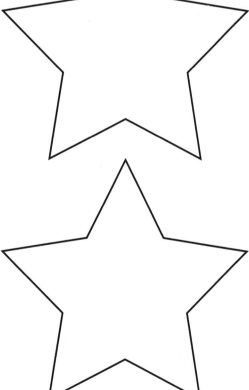

Have each student write and illustrate three wishes.

Unit 8: Over the Rainbow

Journal Writing 3, SV 5799-3

Aa     Zz

Bb
Cc
Dd
Ee
Ff
Gg
Hh
Ii

 Yy
 Xx
Ww
Vv
Uu
Tt
Ss
Rr

_____   _____
_____   _____
_____   _____
_____   _____
_____   _____
_____   _____
_____   _____
_____   _____
_____   _____
_____   _____

Jj Kk Ll Mm Nn Oo Pp Qq

Aa

Bb

Cc

Dd

Ee

Ff

Gg

Hh

Ii

Jj Kk Ll Mm Nn Oo Pp Qq

Zz

Yy

Xx

Ww

Vv

Uu

Tt

Ss

Rr

A a

B b

C c

D d

E e

F f

G g

H h

I i

J j   K k   L l   M m   N n   O o   P p   Q q

Z z

Y y

X x

W w

V v

U u

T t

S s

R r

A a

B b

C c

D d

E e

F f

G g

H h

I i

J j   K k   L l   M m   N n   O o   P p   Q q

Z z

Y y

X x

W w

V v

U u

T t

S s

R r

Name _____ Date _____

A a
B b
C c
D d
E e
F f
G g
H h
I i

J j K k L l M m N n O o P p Q q

Z z
Y y
X x
W w
V v
U u
T t
S s
R r

_____   _____

_____   _____

_____   _____

_____   _____

_____   _____

_____   _____

_____   _____

_____   _____

_____   _____

_____   _____

Journal Writing 3, SV 5799-3

A a

B b

C c

D d

E e

F f

G g

H h

I i

Z z

Y y

X x

W w

V v

U u

T t

S s

R r

J j K k L l M m N n O o P p Q q

A a

B b

C c

D d

E e

F f

G g

H h

I i

J j   K k   L l   M m   N n   O o   P p   Q q

Z z

Y y

X x

W w

V v

U u

T t

S s

R r

_____   _____

_____   _____

_____   _____

_____   _____

_____   _____

_____   _____

_____   _____

_____   _____

_____   _____

_____   _____

_____   _____

Name _____ Date _____

A a   Z z

B b   Y y

C c   X x

D d   _____   _____   W w

E e   _____   _____   V v

F f   _____   _____   U u

G g   _____   _____   T t

Hh   _____   _____   S s

          _____   _____

I i   _____   _____   R r

J j   K k   L l   Mm   N n   O o   P p   Q q

A a

B b

C c

D d

E e

F f

G g

H h

I i

Z z

Y y

X x

W w

V v

U u

T t

S s

R r

J j K k L l M m N n O o P p Q q

_____ _____

_____ _____

_____ _____

_____ _____

_____ _____

_____ _____

_____ _____

_____ _____

_____ _____

_____ _____

A a

B b

C c

D d

E e

F f

G g

H h

I i

J j   K k   L l   M m   N n   O o   P p   Q q

Z z

Y y

X x

W w

V v

U u

T t

S s

R r

80

Journal Writing 3, SV 5799-3

Name _____ Date _____

A a
B b
C c
D d
E e
F f
G g
H h
I i
J j **Kk** L l M m N n O o P p Q q

Z z
Y y
X x
W w
V v
U u
T t
S s
R r

_____ _____

_____ _____

_____ _____

_____ _____

_____ _____

_____ _____

_____ _____

_____ _____

_____ _____

_____ _____

Name _____ Date _____

A a

B b

C c

D d

E e

F f

G g

H h

I i

J j   K k   **L l**   M m   N n   O o   P p   Q q

Z z

Y y

X x

W w

V v

U u

T t

S s

R r

_____   _____

_____   _____

_____   _____

_____   _____

_____   _____

_____   _____

_____   _____

_____   _____

_____   _____

_____   _____

Journal Writing 3, SV 5799-3

Name _____   Date _____

A a

B b

C c

D d

E e

F f

G g

H h

I i

J j   K k   L l   **Mm**   N n   O o   P p   Q q

Z z

Y y

X x

W w

V v

U u

T t

S s

R r

_____   _____

_____   _____

_____   _____

_____   _____

_____   _____

_____   _____

_____   _____

_____   _____

_____   _____

_____   _____

Journal Writing 3, SV 5799-3

A a

B b

C c

D d

E e

F f

G g

H h

I i

J j   K k   L l   M m   **N n**   O o   P p   Q q

Z z

Y y

X x

W w

V v

U u

T t

S s

R r

A a

B b

C c

D d

E e

F f

G g

H h

I i

J j   K k   L l   M m   N n   **O o**   P p   Q q

Z z

Y y

X x

W w

V v

U u

T t

S s

R r

_____   _____

_____   _____

_____   _____

_____   _____

_____   _____

_____   _____

_____   _____

_____   _____

_____   _____

_____   _____

Name _____   Date _____

A a

B b

C c

D d

E e

F f

G g

H h

I i

J j K k L l M m N n O o **P p** Q q

Z z

Y y

X x

W w

V v

U u

T t

S s

R r

_____   _____

_____   _____

_____   _____

_____   _____

_____   _____

_____   _____

_____   _____

_____   _____

_____   _____

_____   _____

A a

B b

C c

D d

E e

F f

G g

H h

I i

J j K k L l M m N n O o P p **Q q**

Z z

Y y

X x

W w

V v

U u

T t

S s

R r

Name _____ Date _____

A a
B b
C c
D d
E e
F f
G g
H h
I i

Z z
Y y
X x
W w
V v
U u
T t
S s
Rr

J j K k L l M m N n O o P p Q q

Name _____ Date _____

A a   Z z

B b   Y y

C c   X x

D d   W w

E e   V v

F f   U u

G g   T t

H h   **S s**

I i   R r

J j K k L l M m N n O o P p Q q

Name _____   Date _____

A a   Z z

B b   Y y

C c   _____   _____   X x

D d   _____   _____   W w

E e   _____   _____   V v

F f   _____   _____   U u

G g   _____   _____   **T t**

H h   _____   _____   S s

I i   _____   _____   R r

J j K k L l  M m N n O o P p Q q

Journal Writing 3, SV 5799-3

Name _____   Date _____

A a

B b

C c

D d

E e

F f

G g

H h

I i

Z z

Y y

X x

W w

V v

Uu

T t

S s

R r

J j   K k   L l   M m   N n   O o   P p   Q q

    Journal Writing 3, SV 5799-3

A a

B b

C c

D d

E e

F f

G g

H h

I i

Z z

Y y

X x

W w

V v

U u

T t

S s

R r

J j   K k   L l   M m   N n   O o   P p   Q q

Name _____   Date _____

A a

B b

C c

D d

E e

F f

G g

H h

I i

J j   K k   L l   M m   N n   O o   P p   Q q

Z z

Y y

X x

W w

V v

U u

T t

S s

R r

Name _____ Date _____

A a

B b

C c

D d

E e

F f

G g

H h

I i

J j   K k   L l   M m   N n   O o   P p   Q q

Z z

Y y

X x

W w

V v

U u

T t

S s

R r

EXIT

6

Name _____ Date _____

A a

B b

C c

D d

E e

F f

G g

H h

I i

J j   K k   L l   M m   N n   O o   P p   Q q

Z z

Y y

X x

W w

V v

U u

T t

S s

R r

A a

B b

C c

D d

E e

F f

G g

H h

I i

J j K k L l M m N n O o P p Q q

Z z

Y y

X x

W w

V v

U u

T t

S s

R r